Baby Goes Home

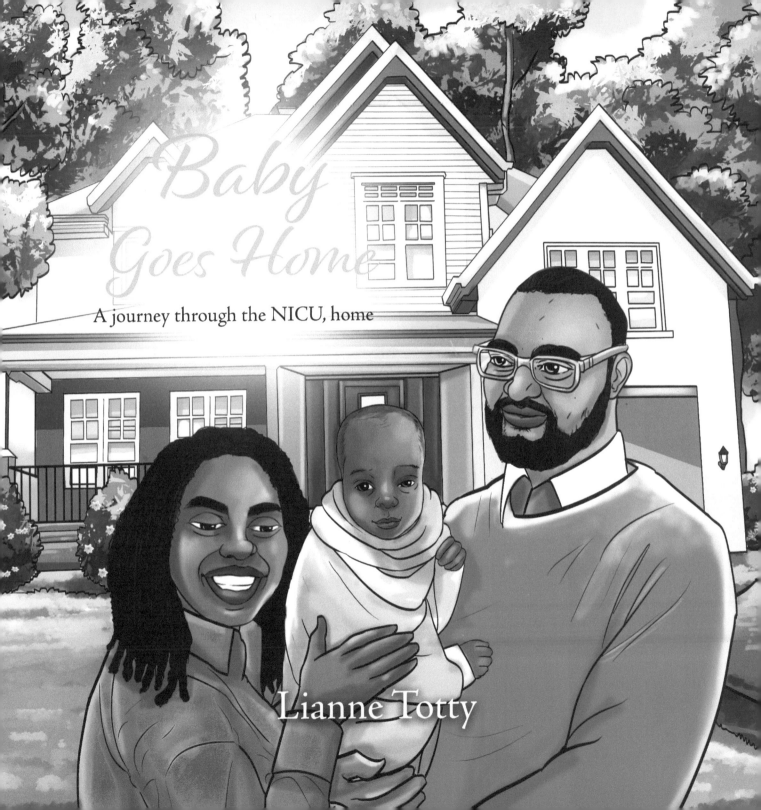

Baby
Goes Home

A journey through the NICU, home

Lianne Totty

Xulon Press
2301 Lucien Way #415
Maitland, FL 32751
407.339.4217
www.xulonpress.com

Printed in the United States of America.

Paperback ISBN-13: 978-1-66280-456-4
Hardcover ISBN-13: 978-1-6628-0457-1

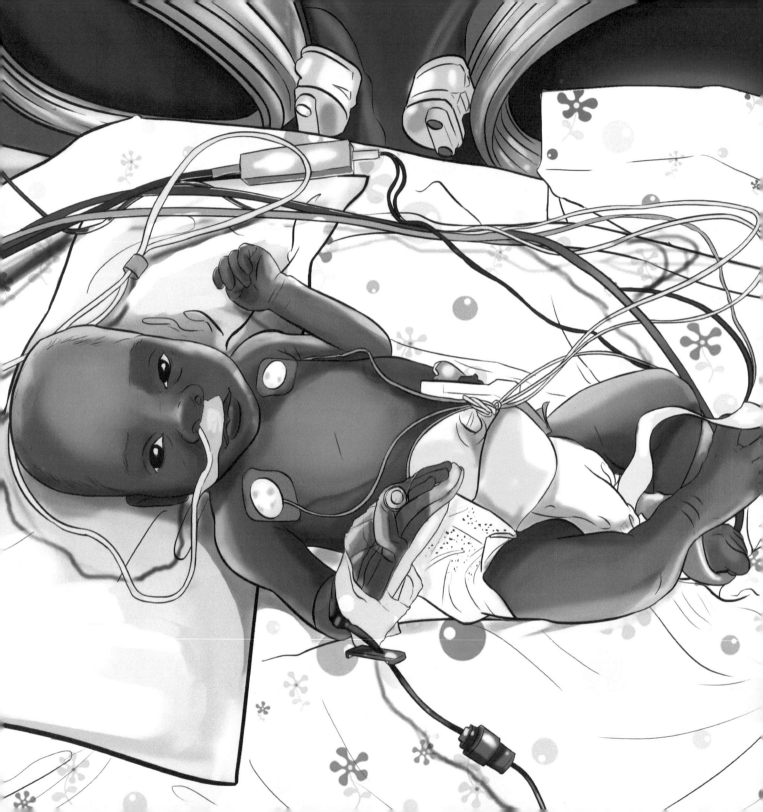

Tiny fingers, tiny toes,
Watch my baby
grow and grow.

Tiny mouth, tiny nose,
I'm so glad it's me
God chose.

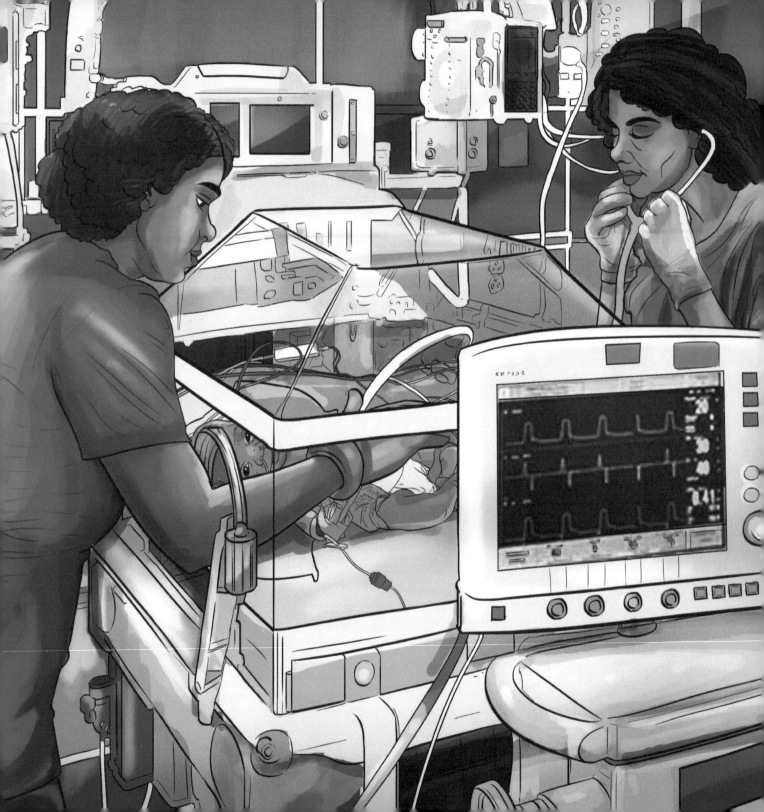

In the NICU, Beep,
Beep, Beep,
Here the little
babies sleep.

All the cords
and all the wires,
Baby's nurses never tire.

Every day we
hope, we pray,
Please, oh please,
let baby stay!

Doctors, nurses,
all the therapists,
Care for baby,
there for his benefit.

After many, many,
many days,
We hear the words
that do amaze.
The doctor comes in with
the nurse and says,

"Go home now
and get some rest!
Come back soon
for the car seat test!"

Tiny fingers, tiny toes,
In a snuggly
wrap he goes.

Tiny mouth and tiny nose,
It's time to take our
baby home!

Some babies are brought home on oxygen.
Some with feeding tubes.
Some babies are brought home with tracheostomies.
While some may have a shunt to help correct brain bleeds.

Some may leave without the sibling that they shared
in the womb.
While others continue to thrive and bloom.

Before they go home, Some babies may need multiple surgeries.
Some need special equipment like heart rate monitor or a nebulizer to help them breathe, while some come home on their own.

Even though some babies might go home with special needs,
In the end those special, strong, warrior babies go home.

Thanks to all the NICU doctors, all the NICU nurses, and all the
NICU staff, in the whole entire world, these wonderful babies get
to go home.

This book is dedicated to the Doctors and staff at MedStar Georgetown University Hospital. They were with us at our lowest low and also at our highest high. Thank you for caring for Líonel and for saving our Lucas, our rainbow, our light.

Author Lianne Totty

Lianne Totty is a children's book author looking to use her past experiences to help others cope . She hopes to help plant the seeds of hope and peace in the hearts of those who have an extended NICU stay ahead or those experienced loss.
Thank you for sharing this experience with her.

Please visit us at www.LianneTotty.com to view more our previous and upcoming titles, purchase more copies and to join our mailing list.

CPSIA information can be obtained
at www.ICGtesting.com
Printed in the USA
LVHW071932250121
677439LV00002B/3